D0825060

Opposite pa...
Magic Kingdo...
Epcot®, the ...
MGM Studio...
Disney's Anim...

There's nothing quite like a personal
moment with Mickey Mouse to create an
unforgettable moment for a small child.

MAGIC KINGDOM® PARK

Wondrous make-believe worlds come to life in the Magic Kingdom® Park, where seven lands of fantasy captivate our imagination. Here, the spirit of Walt Disney lives on, delighting generations with stories and legends shared by all. "May Walt Disney World bring joy and inspiration and new knowledge to all who come to this happy place," said Roy O. Disney on opening day.

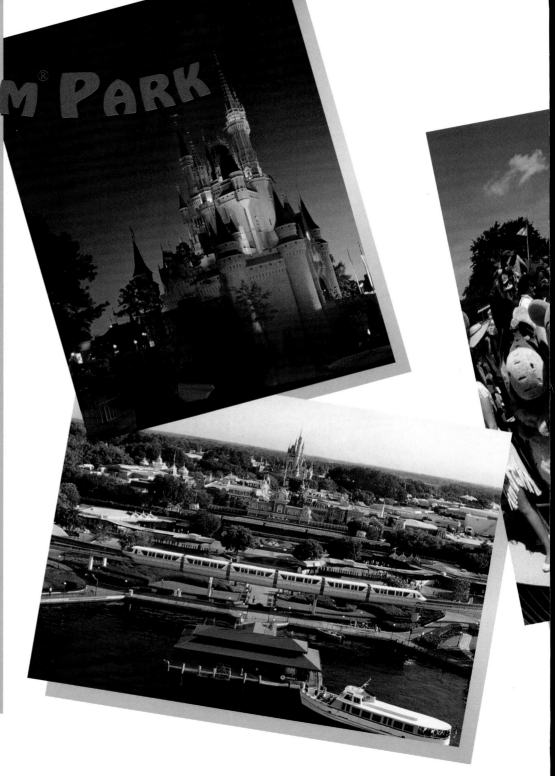

Favorite animated characters come to life, left, greeting guests every day of the year.

The Railroad Station's grand, turn-of-the-century architecture, below, sets the stage for Main Street, U.S.A.

The enchanting Cinderella Castle, top left, looks just like those described in classic fairy tales, but this one's made of steel and fiberglass.

Aerial view, bottom left, shows ferries and monorails that carry millions of visitors every year to the Magic Kingdom® Park.

Main Street U.S.A.

The fantasy begins as you stroll past elaborate Victorian buildings from the era of Walt Disney's early childhood. The sweet harmonies of a barbershop quartet and the clop-clop of horse-drawn streetcars take you back to a gracious, simpler time. Cinderella Castle, soaring 189 feet at the end of the street, leads you to the heart of the Magic Kingdom® Park.

4

Main Street U.S.A. provides guests with a broad range of marvelous shopping opportunities, left.

Gingerbread architecture, period lighting fixtures, and beautiful baskets of flowers recreate a small-town Main Street.

You can see the first sound cartoon, *Steamboat Willie*, starring Mickey Mouse, in the Main Street Cinema, above.

Old-fashioned horse-drawn trolleys, right, carry guests the length of Main Street, U.S.A.

5

Adventureland

Lush landscaping—vivid bougainvillea, hibiscus, ferns, and flowering vines—along with the sound of beating drums lead the way to this great escape to the exotic islands of the Caribbean, Polynesia, and Southeast Asia. Adventures await as you journey down mysterious rivers, face off with fierce pirates, or climb to the top of a perfect treehouse.

The themed bridge, above, wrapped with tropical flowers and vines, leads the way to this exotic land.

Realistic wood carvings near the Jungle Cruise, left, are a perfect backdrop for humorous souvenir photos.

An engaging skipper takes you on the trip of a lifetime on the Jungle Cruise, far left, where you'll spy bathing elephants, zebras, giraffes, lions, vultures, and even a few headhunters. Cambodian temple ruins, left, are along the way.

The Tropical Serenade, below far left, was among the first Disney attractions, featuring more than 200 birds, flowers, and tiki god statues. Center left, are some of the feathered stars of the show. The Swiss Family Treehouse has plenty of room for wandering guests, center, with realistic props like the writing table, below.

Pirates raid a Caribbean town, and you get a front-row seat for all of the action in this popular boat ride.

A parrot dressed in a pirate costume, below center, greets riders at the attraction's entrance. Pirates turn the town upside down in elaborate scenes like those below.

Liberty Square

ome face to face with every U.S. president and 999 grinning ghosts as you're transported to Colonial America in this patriotic village with clapboard and brick buildings, brightly colored gardens, and an authentic paddle-wheel steamboat churning through the Rivers of America.

A majestic, 135-year-old live oak, above, is hung with 13 lanterns to recall the original colonies. A fife and drum corps, left, performs daily.

9

The mood is light-hearted in the Haunted Mansion, full of special effects like spooky dancing and dining specters, above, with music provided by a transparent organ player, right. A spirited graveyard, left, is just one stop along the way. The old house was built to resemble estates in the Hudson River Valley that were built by the Dutch in the 18th century.

The Liberty Square Riverboat, top, is a real steam-powered sternwheeler that offers a relaxing, picturesque cruise on the Rivers of America.

President Bill Clinton gets a speaking role in The Hall of Presidents, above, where all 42 chief executives are on stage.

FRONTIERLAND

FRONTIER TRADING POST

"TEXAS" JOHN SLAUGHTER - TRAIL BOSS

Ghost towns and boom-towns of the Old West come to life in this re-creation of the American frontier, with wooden sidewalks and desertlike landscaping. Two of the most thrilling Magic Kingdom® attractions, Splash Mountain and Big Thunder Mountain Railroad, are here, as well as one of the most charming spots in the entire park, Tom Sawyer Island.

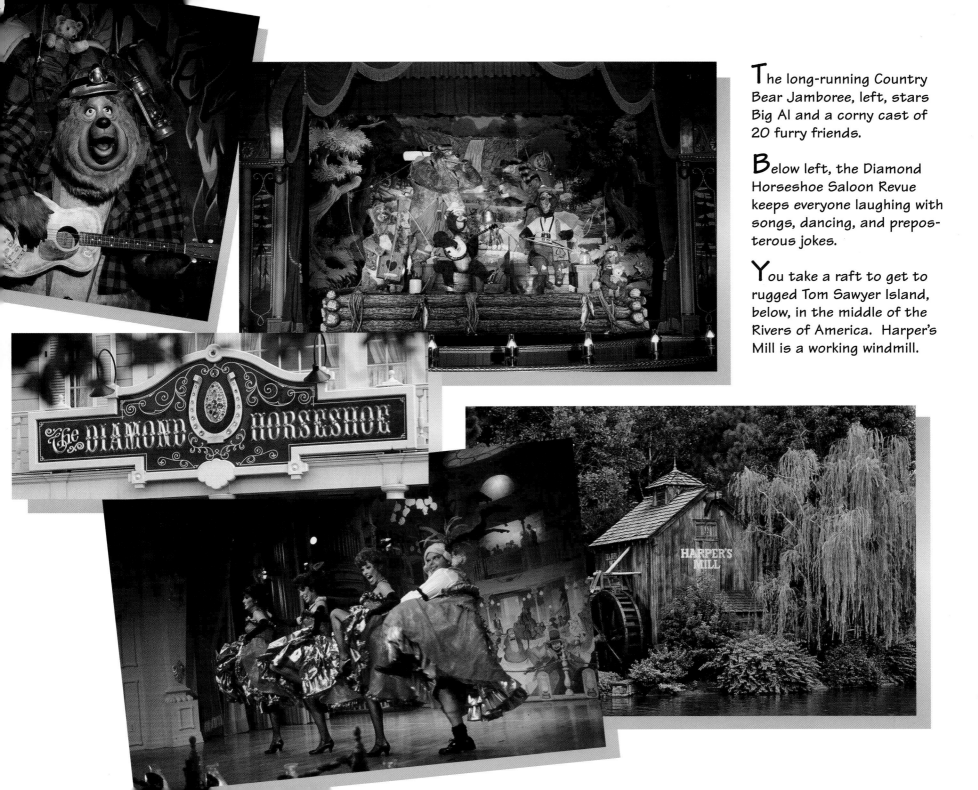

The long-running Country Bear Jamboree, left, stars Big Al and a corny cast of 20 furry friends.

Below left, the Diamond Horseshoe Saloon Revue keeps everyone laughing with songs, dancing, and preposterous jokes.

You take a raft to get to rugged Tom Sawyer Island, below, in the middle of the Rivers of America. Harper's Mill is a working windmill.

13

Runaway mine cars take a thrilling spin with plenty of swoops and curves on Big Thunder Mountain Railroad. The Southwestern landscape is reminiscent of Arizona's Monument Valley.

The mines at Big Thunder are said to be haunted, the trains move swiftly around the mountain as if some supernatural force were pushing them.

On Splash Mountain, based on the award-winning film *Song of the South*, you can take the plunge with Brer Rabbit and friends.

The biggest drop is 52 feet, with a top speed of 40 miles per hour, making it the steepest flume in the world.

15

Fantasyland

Walt Disney called this the happiest land of all, a place where you can step into the pages of a giant storybook of attractions based on the classic Disney animated tales. Fly with Dumbo, take a spin on Cinderella's Golden Carrousel, or share a hug with Ariel...dreams do come true.

Cinderella Castle murals, far right, contain jewellike pieces of Italian glass, some fused with silver and 14-carat gold.

A delicate bronze statue of Cinderella, inset, is just outside the castle doors. Nighttime view of Cinderella Castle, right.

Peter Pan's Flight

The dwarfs are often around for a hug at Snow White's Adventures, above.

You're whisked above the action in a flying version of Captain Hook's ornate ship on Peter Pan's Flight, left.

Snow White's
Adventures, far left, creates a sense that you are
actually riding through
the motion picture.

Mr. Toad's Wild Ride,
left and above, is a
rowdy adventure along
the road to Nowhere in
Particular with Mr. J.
Thaddeus Toad.

19

The aerial view, left, shows the Skyway to Tomorrowland tram high above Fantasyland.

Cinderella's Golden Carrousel, middle right, is the oldest Magic Kingdom® attraction, built in 1917 for Detroit's Palace Garden Park. On board are 72 horses, no two exactly alike.

Dumbo, The Flying Elephant, far right top, takes riders for a memorable spin above Fantasyland.

Far right bottom, the oversized teacups of the Mad Tea Party, inspired by *Alice in Wonderland*, whirl and spin wildly, much to the joy of the riders.

The Sword in the Stone, left, won't budge until Merlin the Magician makes his daily appearance and grants powers of strength to a lucky youngster.

Puppetry, special effects, animation, and music are used in Legend of the Lion King to bring to life favorite characters from the animated classic, The Lion King.

Hundreds of dolls sing and dance in It's a Small World, originally created for the 1964-65 New York World's Fair.

Tiny Polynesian dancers, a crooning crocodile, and Dutch children in wooden shoes, insets, all sing along to the attraction's unforgettable melody.

23

Mickey's Toontown Fair

Mickey Mouse and all his toon pals greet you in this whimsical village set amidst clusters of candy-striped tents and fanciful fairgrounds, where kid-favorite attractions recall the old-fashioned excitement of a county fair. Bring your autograph book— the characters are there all day long, welcoming old friends and making new ones!

Favorite Disney characters, above, take center stage at Mickey's Toontown Fair.

Lily pads spout jumping streams and spray without warning, right, on Donald Duck's Boat, Miss Daisy.

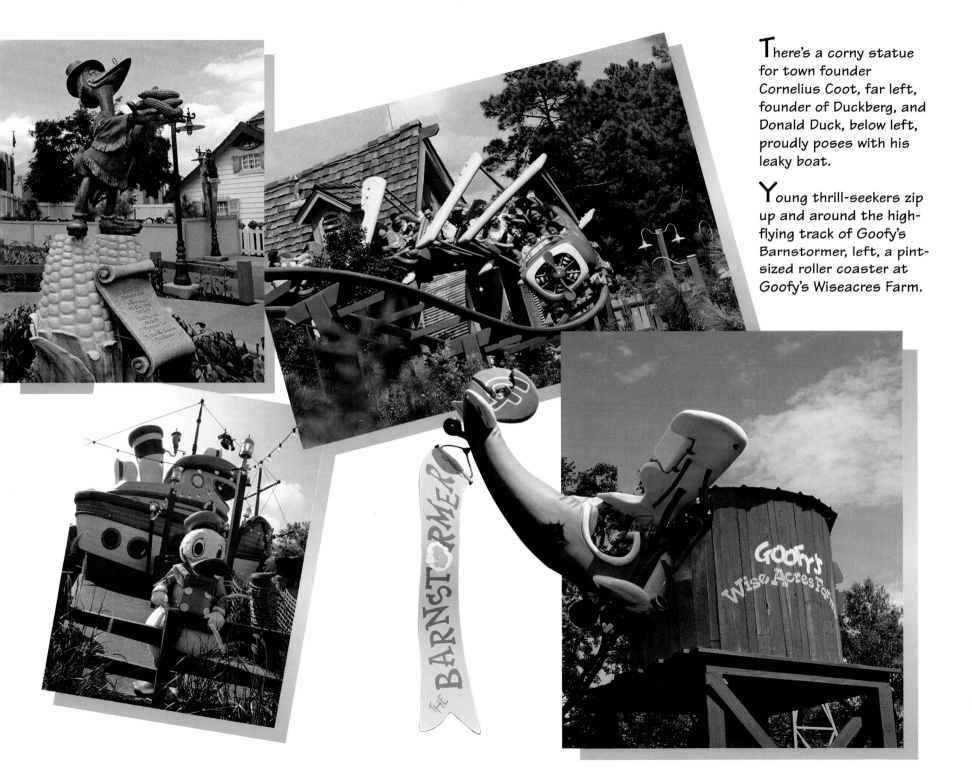

There's a corny statue for town founder Cornelius Coot, far left, founder of Duckberg, and Donald Duck, below left, proudly poses with his leaky boat.

Young thrill-seekers zip up and around the high-flying track of Goofy's Barnstormer, left, a pint-sized roller coaster at Goofy's Wiseacres Farm.

25

Tomorrowland

You can experience the future that never was in this fantasy city from the science fiction stories of Jules Verne and H. G. Wells. Shiny robots do the work, planet-hopping rocket ships battle aliens, and a time-machine journey through the ages becomes a thrilling reality along the Avenue of the Planets. Fantastic intergalactic adventures await!

Sky-piercing beacons and glistening metal illuminated by neon set the stage in this friendly, future-town neighborhood, where even the palm trees, above, are stylized.

A whole cast of zany new characters inhabits this future city, like Sunny Eclipse, far left, a "lounge singer" in Cosmic Rays Starlight Café.

27

The Timekeeper, opposite page, is an adventure to centuries past and those yet to come, with your hosts 9-Eye and Timekeeper.

There's a hideous creature on the loose, with chilling special effects to make The ExtraTERRORestrial Alien Encounter the scariest Magic Kingdom® attraction.

X·S TECH

NOW ON EARTH

Alien Encounter

29

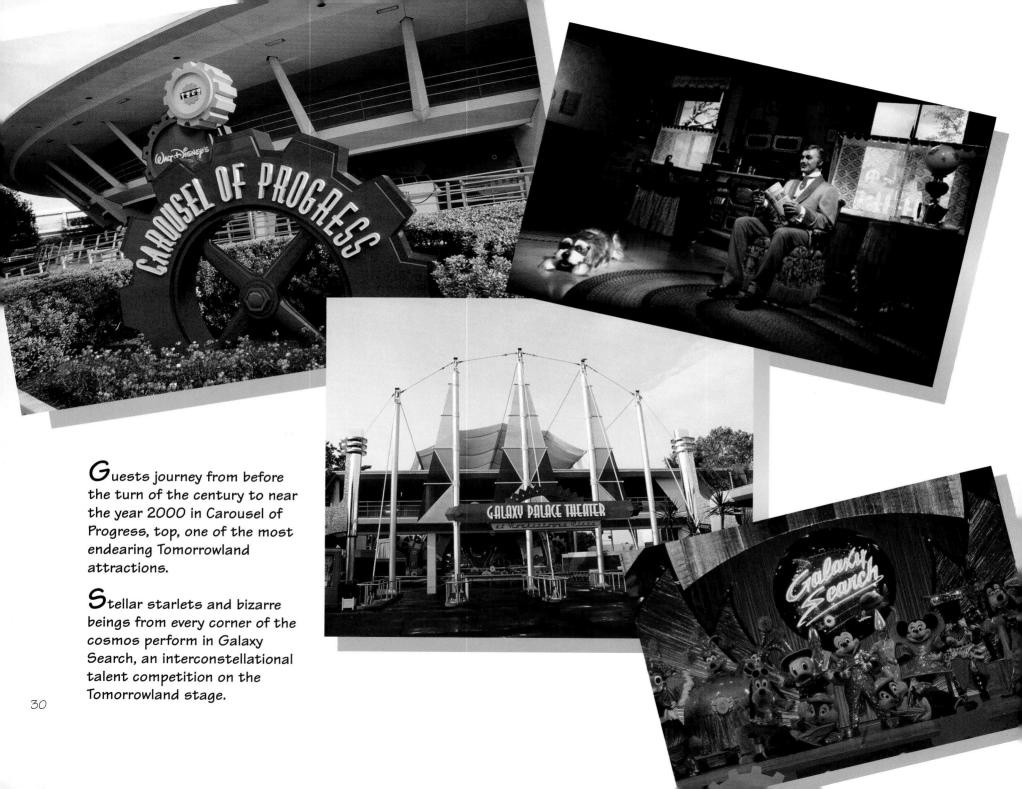

Guests journey from before the turn of the century to near the year 2000 in Carousel of Progress, top, one of the most endearing Tomorrowland attractions.

Stellar starlets and bizarre beings from every corner of the cosmos perform in Galaxy Search, an interconstellational talent competition on the Tomorrowland stage.

Hop aboard Astro Orbiter's machine-age rockets for a quick swing through space surrounded by whirling planets.

This distinctive white structure is the home of Space Mountain, a roller-coaster ride in darkness with shooting stars and flashing lights.

The thrill of climbing behind the wheel of your very own car happens at an early age at Grand Prix Raceway, above and right.

Take Flight, far right, is a lighthearted look at the history of flying, including whimsical scenes from the earliest days of aviation and a bird's-eye view of Paris rooftops.

Nightime Magic

The fantasy doesn't end when the sun sets, as the Magic Kingdom® Park comes to life with spectacular evening shows. Thousands of lights twinkle on Main Street, U.S.A., and brilliant fireworks explode in the skies above Cinderella Castle. Even the surrounding Bay Lake is ablaze with Disney's magical creatures, both sweet and surreal .

Dazzling Spectro-Magic is created with about 600,000 miniature lights that move in perfect concert with sound effects.

The Sparkling Electrical Water Pageant is a nightly parade of floating creatures on Bay Lake.

Cinderella Castle is all aglow as the Fantasy in the Sky fireworks display, right, lights up the night.

"EPCOT® FUTURE WORLD"

There's something new around every corner at Epcot, Disney's "Discovery Park." Future World features some of the newest and most intriguing ideas in science and technology. A showplace for man's achievements past, present, and future, this ever-changing environment both inspires and entertains its guests.

Silver-colored Spaceship Earth, the 180-foot-high geosphere that is the symbol of Epcot®, creates a dramatic backdrop.

Alec Tronic, far left, delivers comic one-liners and a lesson in Audio-Animatronic technology from a stage in Innoventions.

Innoventions' bright neon lights up Future World, left, pointing the way to this interactive technology playground in the heart of Epcot. Guests are surrounded by exciting shows and interactive displays that make technology fun.

SPACESHIP EARTH

This amazing trip through the history of communication starts with cave men, above, and includes glimpses of the start of theater in ancient Greece, left, and a look at the Romans' pioneering system of roads, opposite page.

The Global Neighborhood, above and far left, lets you try out fantastic new technologies as you end your Spaceship Earth journey.

A spectacular nighttime view of the world's only 16-million-pound geosphere, left.

39

HORIZONS

Horizons looks into the achievable future and takes you on an exciting exploration of options for living and working in the 21st century.

Domestic robots envisioned in the 1930s and 1940s, inset, recall the often-hilarious views of yesterday's future.

UNIVERSE OF ENERGY

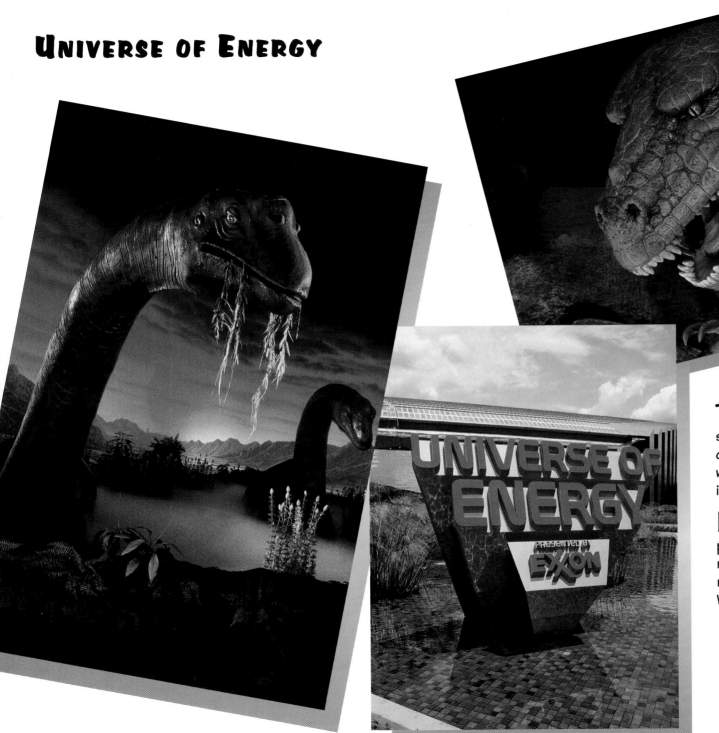

Two acres of rooftop solar panels, left, help operate this attraction, which is all about the importance of energy.

Lifelike dinosaurs in a primeval world, above, make this one of the most popular Future World attractions.

41

WONDERS OF LIFE

The spiraling sculpture in front of this gold-domed pavilion is a seven-story replica of the DNA molecule.

Many attractions devoted to health and fitness are offered within the spacious interior of the 100,000-square-foot building, inset.

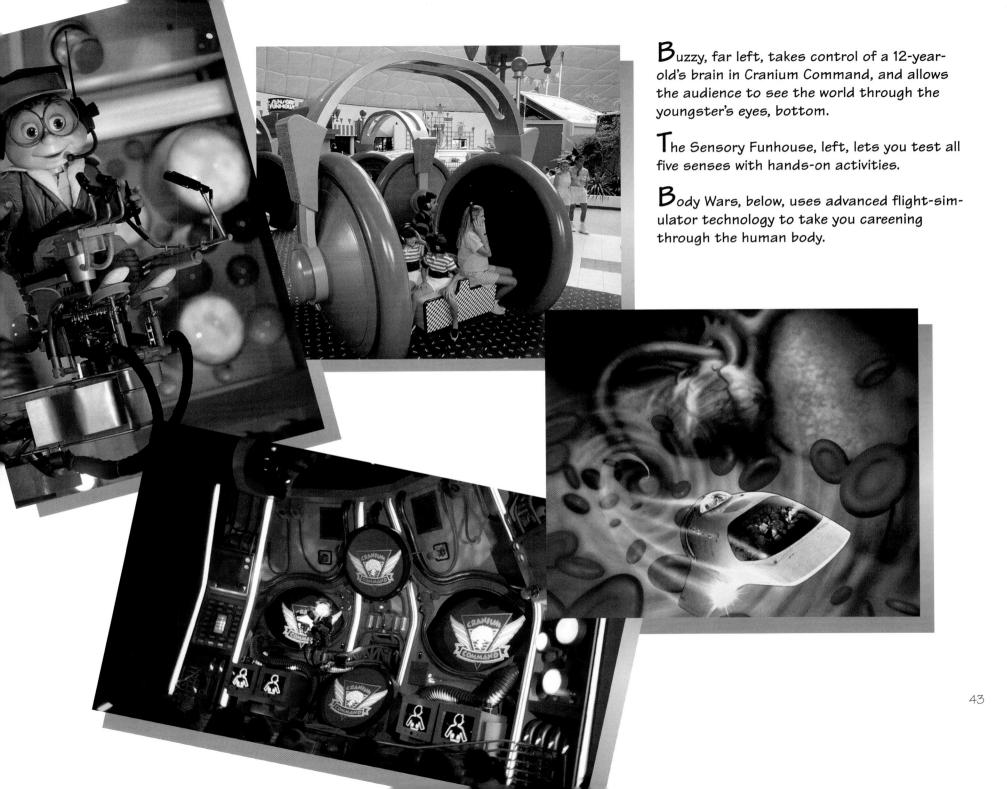

Buzzy, far left, takes control of a 12-year-old's brain in Cranium Command, and allows the audience to see the world through the youngster's eyes, bottom.

The Sensory Funhouse, left, lets you test all five senses with hands-on activities.

Body Wars, below, uses advanced flight-simulator technology to take you careening through the human body.

TEST TRACK

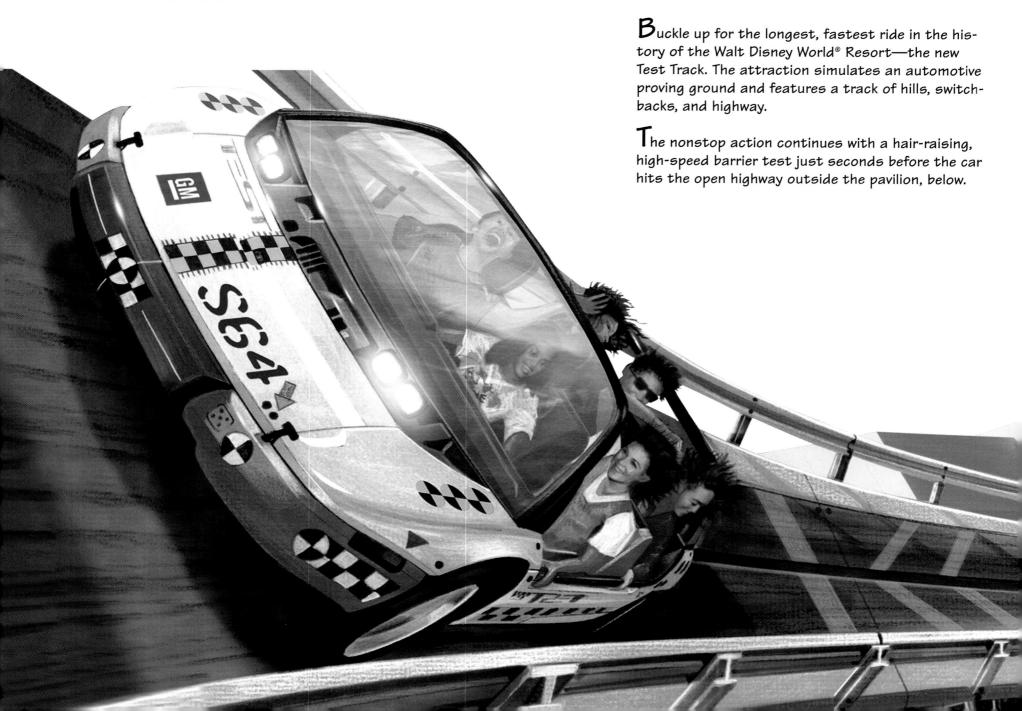

Buckle up for the longest, fastest ride in the history of the Walt Disney World® Resort—the new Test Track. The attraction simulates an automotive proving ground and features a track of hills, switchbacks, and highway.

The nonstop action continues with a hair-raising, high-speed barrier test just seconds before the car hits the open highway outside the pavilion, below.

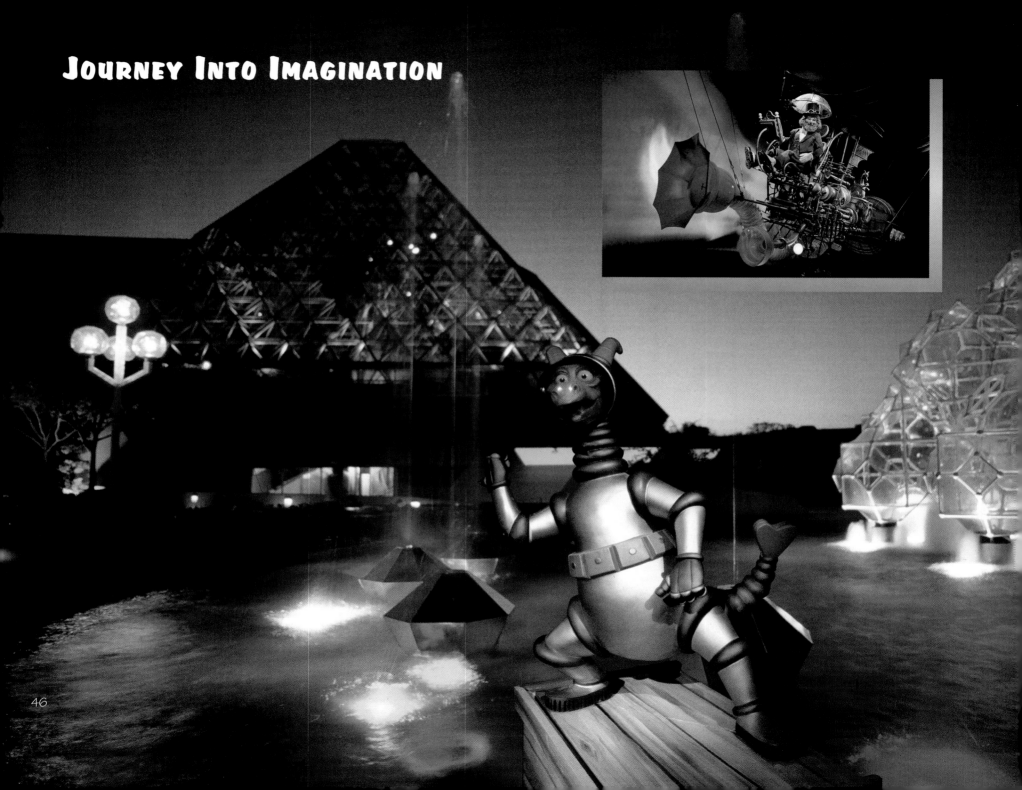

JOURNEY INTO IMAGINATION

You won't believe your eyes—or your size—in Honey, I Shrunk the Audience, a 3-D adventure with realistic special effects that will leave you squealing and squirming in your seat.

Jolly, red-headed Dreamfinder and his baby dragon Figment take you on a whimsical journey into the world of imagination, where you encounter scenes like those above. Image Works, middle photo, is full of fun, like this neon Rainbow Corridor.

47

THE LAND

This airy pavilion takes a look at the foods we eat, with a fascinating boat ride through greenhouses displaying crops from around the world.

Parodies of classic rock 'n' roll songs teach a humorous lesson about good nutrition in "Food Rocks," below.

THE LIVING SEAS

The mysteries of the deep blue ocean are unraveled in this pavilion, which contains 4,000 sea creatures.

You can get close-up views through crystal-clear windows of divers, dolphins, and even an underwater Mickey Mouse.

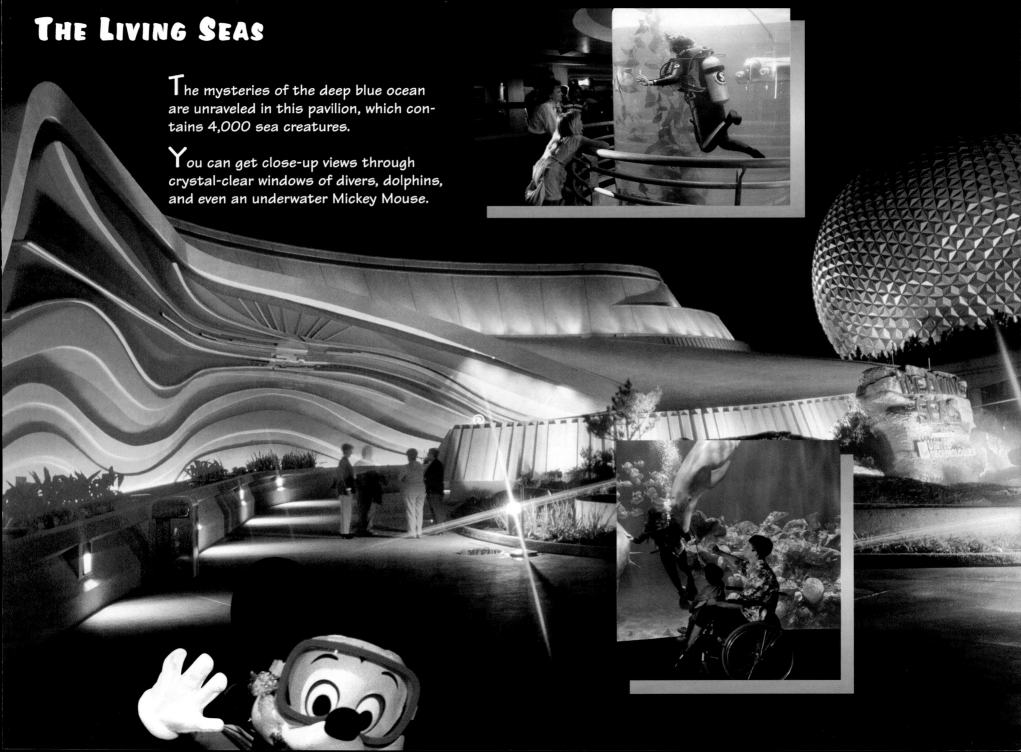

EPCOT® WORLD SHOWCASE

A kaleidoscope of fascinating experiences await in this microcosm of international cultures. Eleven nations side by side present historic scenes familiar to world travelers: buildings, streets, gardens, and monuments are designed to give Epcot guests an authentic experience in each pavilion. Exotic cuisine, entertainment, and artisans complete the fantasy trip around the globe.

Canada's 19th-century-style French château left, marks the transition from Future World to World Showcase.

The distinctive architecture paints an interesting picture—Japan, Morocco, and France are shown below.

NORWAY

Distinctive Norwegian architecture, above, includes a stave church and a castle styled after Akershus, a 14th-century fortress that stands in Oslo's harbor.

The exciting Maelstrom ride, above right, is a fantasy voyage full of surprises, including these trolls in a mythical Norwegian forest, right.

CHINA

A replica of Beijing's Temple of Heaven, right, is actually a theater offering a breathtaking film of some of China's rarest sites.

The sights and sounds of China are authentically re-created with live performances, bottom inset.

GERMANY

Fairy-tale architecture and exuberant entertainers whisk you away to an imaginary German village.

Rousing oompah music and hearty German foods in the pavilion's vast Biergarten, bottom left, create a festive atmosphere.

ITALY

Fanciful re-creations of Venice include the bell tower topped with a gold-leafed angel, right, just like the one in the real St. Mark's Square.

Characters from Disney's *Pinocchio*, below, join real-life entertainers, center, in the pavilion's piazza.

AMERICAN ADVENTURE

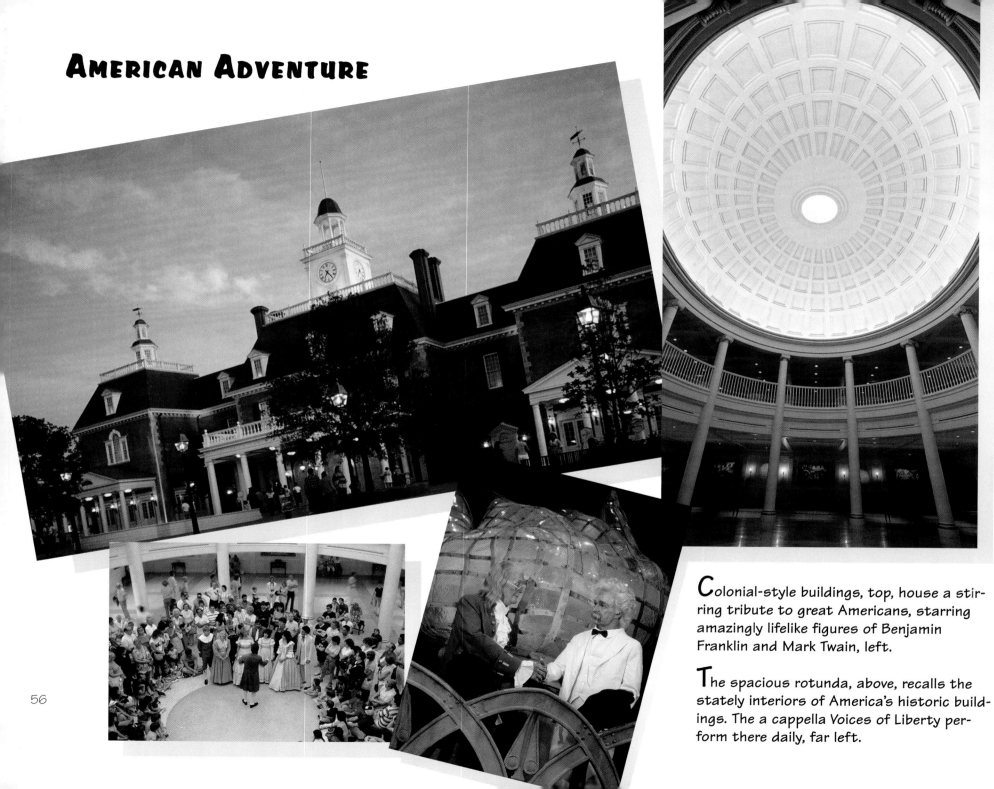

Colonial-style buildings, top, house a stirring tribute to great Americans, starring amazingly lifelike figures of Benjamin Franklin and Mark Twain, left.

The spacious rotunda, above, recalls the stately interiors of America's historic buildings. The a cappella Voices of Liberty perform there daily, far left.

JAPAN

A bright red torii gate welcomes you to Japan, with authentic cuisine in teppanyaki rooms, inset above. Ancient drama, below, brings centuries of culture to life, while details such as the lamp, inset right, produce the proper atmosphere.

MOROCCO

Lively dancers and musicians chant the haunting folk songs of Morocco in the courtyard, top.

The intricately carved Koutoubia Minaret, above left and right, stands guard over the pavilion's entrance. The busy street market, left, sells authentic Moroccan wares.

FRANCE

Bonjour! Paris in all its glory is re-created with the Eiffel Tower, above right, rising above it all. A fabulous French restaurant, delectable French pastries, lovely shops, and a spectacular motion picture filled with the country's beauty complete the journey.

UNITED KINGDOM

Entertainers draw you into the neighborhood with their bawdy British humor, below, where Tudor, Victorian, and Georgian buildings line the cobblestone streets.

Colorful, well-tended gardens, left and right, offer plenty of space for a quiet moment.

CANADA

From rustic totem poles to ornate French architecture, this pavilion showcases the western hemisphere's largest nation.

Lively entertainment outdoors, left, and a motion picture inside the pavilion offer a glimpse of our neighbor to the north.

ILLUMINATIONS

Music, intense fireworks, fountains, lights, and lasers create a spectacular nighttime show on the World Showcase Lagoon.

From left, Canada, Germany, United Kingdom, China, and France are trimmed with twinkling lights for the extravaganza.

63

DISNEY-MGM STUDIOS

It's "cine-magic!" From the moment guests enter the world's most celebrated movie park, they feel as if they have strolled into the middle of the action, starting with the dreamy era of Tinseltown of the '30s and '40s, then fast-forwarding to showcase some of today's hottest films and TV shows in action-packed attractions.

Hollywood Boulevard, Great Movie Ride

Hollywood Boulevard, above, is inspired by Tinseltown's "Golden Age," with the famous Chinese Theatre and other landmarks side by side.

Fantasy, intrigue, and adventure await guests on The Great Movie Ride, right, with lifelike scenes from memorable films.

The TwiLiGHT ZONE
TowER of TERRoR®

The spooky Hollywood Tower Hotel looms 199 feet above the Disney-MGM Studios, the perfect setting for a terrifying adventure.

The plummet is 13 stories and the fright is unforgettable, with not one but two heart-stopping drops in pitch darkness, inset.

The HOLLYWOOD TOWER Hotel

"The Twilight Zone" is a registered trademark of CBS, Inc.

BACKSTAGE STUDIO TOUR, NEW YORK STREET

All aboard for an insider's look at the magic of movie-making, including big-city street scenes, below.

Special-effects disasters, including floods and an earthquake, are a surprise for guests in Catastrophe Canyon, left.

BEAUTY AND THE BEAST, VOYAGE OF THE LITTLE MERMAID

The mesmerizing tale of *Beauty and the Beast* comes alive in an extravagant stage show, left and below.

A colorful cast of characters tells the story of *The Little Mermaid*, below left.

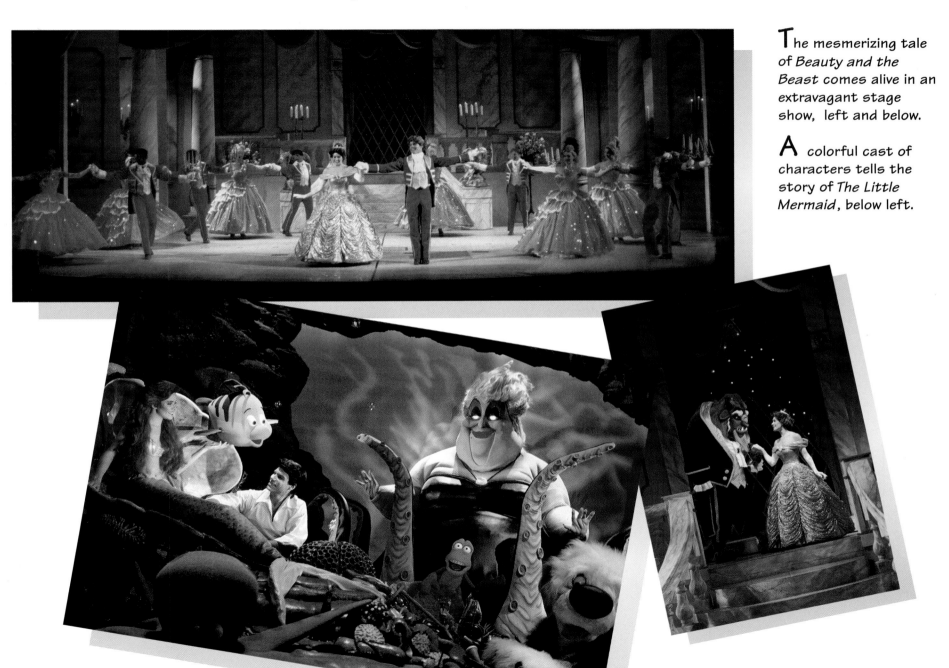

69

STAR TOURS

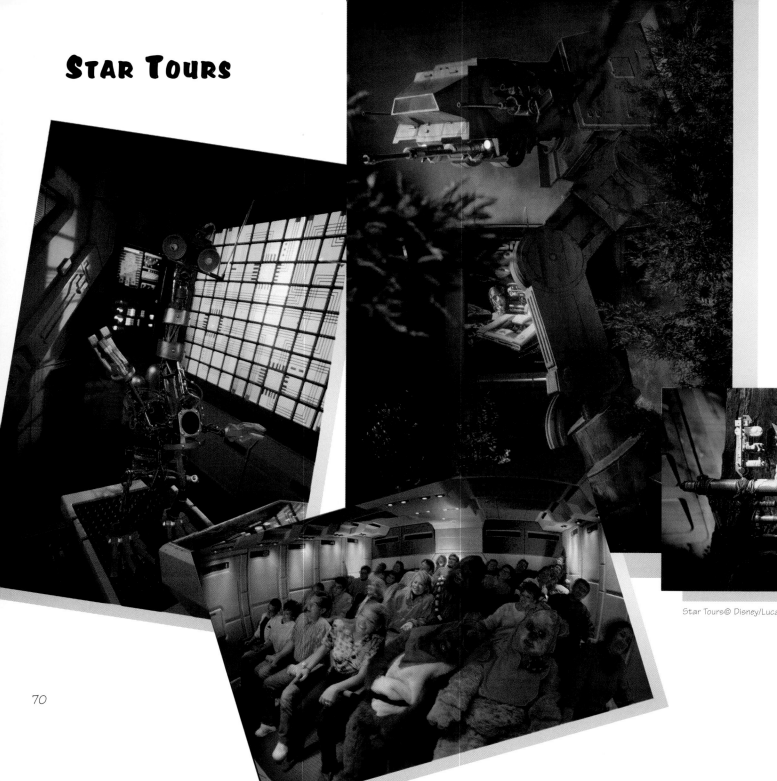

This wild journey transports you on an uproarious flight to the Moon of Endor. Droids, far left, welcome everyone aboard after a walk through an Ewok Village, left. Endor Vendors, below, is the final stop for galactic goodies.

Star Tours© Disney/Lucasfilm Ltd.   Star Wars is a trademark of Lucasfilm Ltd.

INDIANA JONES EPIC STUNT SPECTACULAR

Edge-of-your-seat scenes from *Raiders of the Lost Ark* come to life in this fast-paced stunt show, with volunteers selected from the audience at the beginning of the show to participate as extras.

Indiana Jones™ Epic Stunt Spectacular © Disney/Lucasfilm Ltd.
Indiana Jones is a trademark of Lucasfilm Ltd.

71

Superstar Television, ABC Sound Studio

Scenes from your favorite TV shows are right before your eyes, below, and you may get a chance to try out your acting talents!

Ever wonder how sound effects are created for a film? Audiences find out, with hilarious results, bottom.

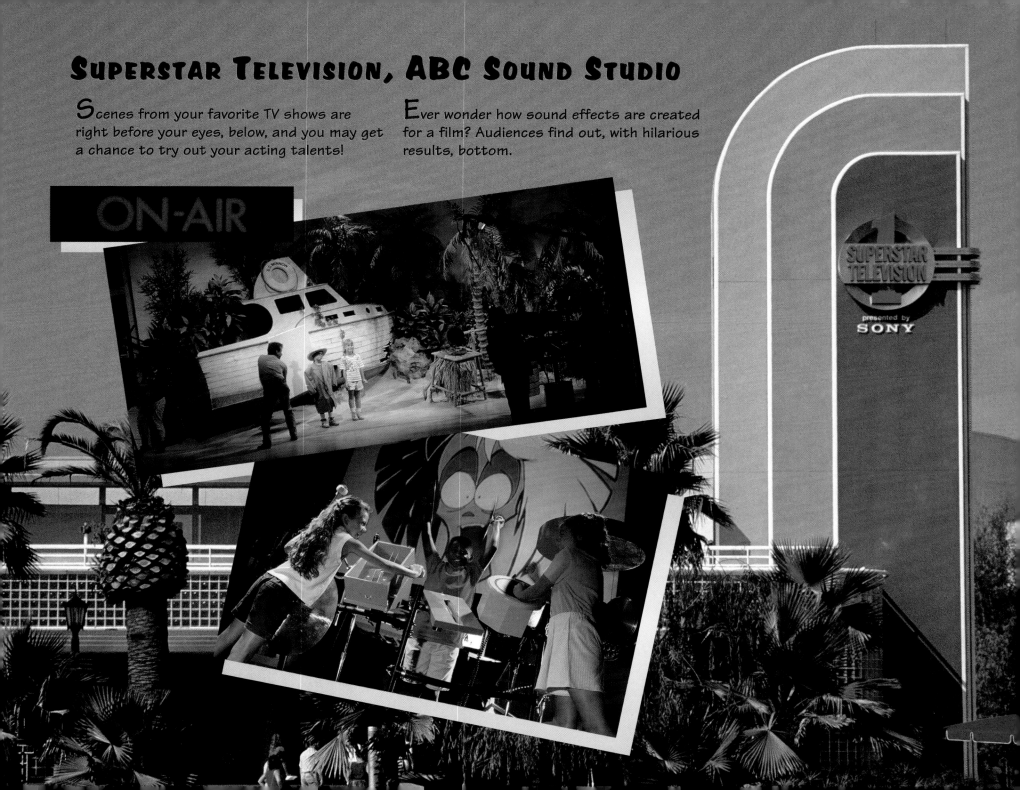

HONEY I SHRUNK THE KIDS MOVIE SET ADVENTURE, JIM HENSON'S MUPPETVISION 3D

Y ou'll experience what it feels like to be the size of an ant in the "Honey" playground, top left and above.

E xplosive in-theater effects and amazing 3-D action showcase the wild antics of Jim Henson's legendary Muppet characters, left.

MUPPET★VISION 3D

PRESENTED BY

Kodak

©1997 The Jim Henson Company

THE MAGIC OF DISNEY ANIMATION

This is the only animation studio in the world that features a visitor tour. Thousands of theme park guests get a peek at the work on Disney's latest films through the studio's glass-walled corridor.

DINING AT THE STUDIOS

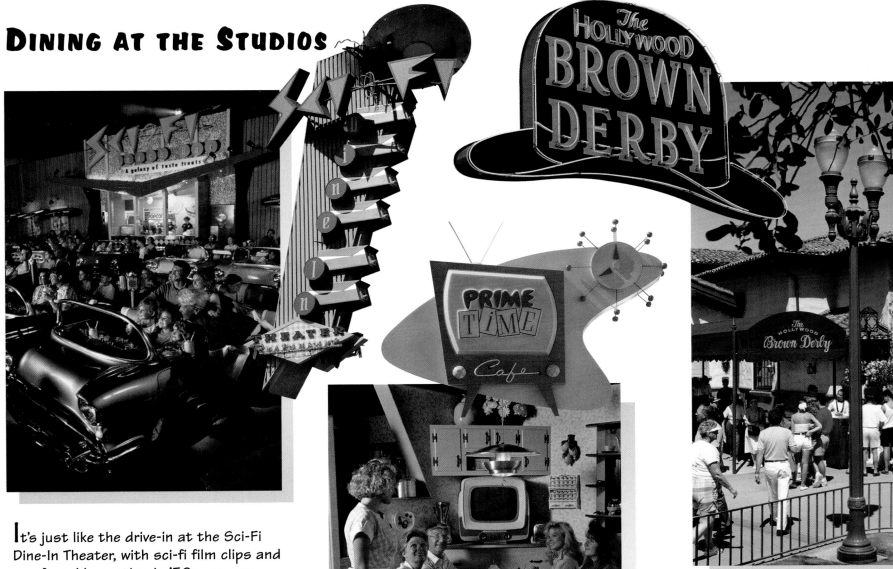

It's just like the drive-in at the Sci-Fi Dine-In Theater, with sci-fi film clips and comfortable seating in '50s-era convertibles.

Sit at the kitchen table and give "mom" your order while you watch TV in the '50s Prime Time Café, right.

The chic atmosphere of the original Hollywood Brown Derby is re-created in this upscale eatery, above.

75

THE REST OF THE WORLD

So many incredible ideas have become reality, bringing seemingly endless entertainment options to millions of Walt Disney World® vacationers. Water parks, nightlife, golf courses, wildly divergent resorts...the ideas just keep coming. As Walt Disney once said, "There's enough land here to hold all the ideas and plans we can possibly imagine."

DISNEY'S TYPHOON LAGOON AND DISNEY'S BLIZZARD BEACH

It may look like an abandoned ski resort, but the "snowy" slopes are really water slides at Blizzard Beach, inset left.

You can snorkel with live sharks and colorful fish in Shark Reef at Typhoon Lagoon, below, one of the many highlights of this action-packed water park.

DISNEY'S DISCOVERY ISLAND

Get up close with nature at this delightful island zoo, originally envisioned by Walt Disney himself as a refuge for animals. You can see about 130 species of wildlife, with many animals running free.

Disney's Grand Floridian Beach Resort & Spa

Disney's "crown jewel," inspired by grand, turn-of-the-century seaside resorts, is on the shores of the Seven Seas Lagoon. The palatial lobby, below, soars five stories with stained-glass domes.

DISNEY'S CONTEMPORARY RESORT

The beautiful, ultramodern convention center, left and above, gracefully blends with the original resort.

Sleek monorails glide through the A-frame, right, with a huge, floor-to-ceiling tile mural of Native American children in the cavernous lobby, far right.

DISNEY'S POLYNESIAN RESORT

Fabulous landscaping and a laid-back atmosphere make this resort on the shores of the Seven Seas Lagoon a longtime favorite.

Minnie entertains at Mickey's Tropical Revue, left. Family-style dinners, roasted over an open fire, are served at O'Hana, below.

81

DISNEY'S FORT WILDERNESS RESORT AND CAMPGROUND, RIVER COUNTRY

After dark, there's a nightly campfire, above, or an evening at the comical Hoop-Dee-Doo Musical Revue, bottom right.

There's plenty of action, with Disney's River Country Water Park, above right, and horseback riding on wilderness trails, right.

DISNEY'S WILDERNESS LODGE

The grandeur of America's national parks is the inspiration for this beautiful resort, created with tons of granite flagstone and hundreds of giant lodgepole pines from the West. The resort features a volcanic meadow with bubbling color pools and geysers spewing misty streams up to 100 feet in the air, bottom left. The lobby, bottom right, features two 55-foot, hand-carved totem poles.

DISNEY'S DIXIE LANDINGS RESORT, DISNEY'S PORT ORLEANS RESORT

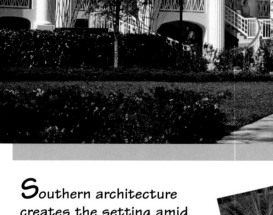

Southern architecture creates the setting amid trees and flowers for these two charming resorts.

The Doubloon Lagoon pool at Disney's Port Orleans Resort, right, is built around a fanciful, curving sea serpent. Alligators add to the whimsy, far right.

DISNEY'S CARIBBEAN BEACH RESORT

It's a make-believe escape to the Caribbean at this carefree resort, with its brilliant, sun-washed colors and white-sand beaches. Five island-themed villages surround Old Port Royale, a stone-walled complex for dining, water recreation, and shopping.

DISNEY'S YACHT AND BEACH CLUB RESORTS

The grand, turn-of-the-century seaside resorts of New England are recalled at this gracious location, set on a 25-acre lake. Far left, a nighttime view of the meandering Stormalong Bay, the resort's incredible swimming area. An elegant convention center, below, is part of Disney's Yacht Club Resort.

DISNEY'S BOARDWALK RESORT

The carefree fun of the 1930s mid-Atlantic coast is captured at this waterfront village, which includes its own entertainment district, left.

The Flying Fish Café, above, is among the delicious dining opportunities on the Boardwalk.

DOWNTOWN DISNEY WEST SIDE

This sizzling showplace heats up with, inset from left, the House of Blues™, Forty Thirst Street for espresso and fresh juice drinks, Bongos Cuban Cafe™, and the Wolfgang Puck® Cafe.

DOWNTOWN DISNEY PLEASURE ISLAND

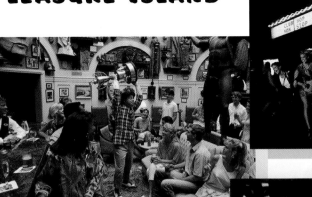

F avorite nightspots at Pleasure Island include the Adventurers Club, above left; Mannequins Dance Palace, above center; and West End Stage, above right.

DOWNTOWN DISNEY MARKETPLACE

T he Marketplace is a shopper's dream, with exciting restaurants like Rainforest Cafe, above, and the world's largest Disney character store, World of Disney, right.

DISNEY'S ALL-STAR RESORTS

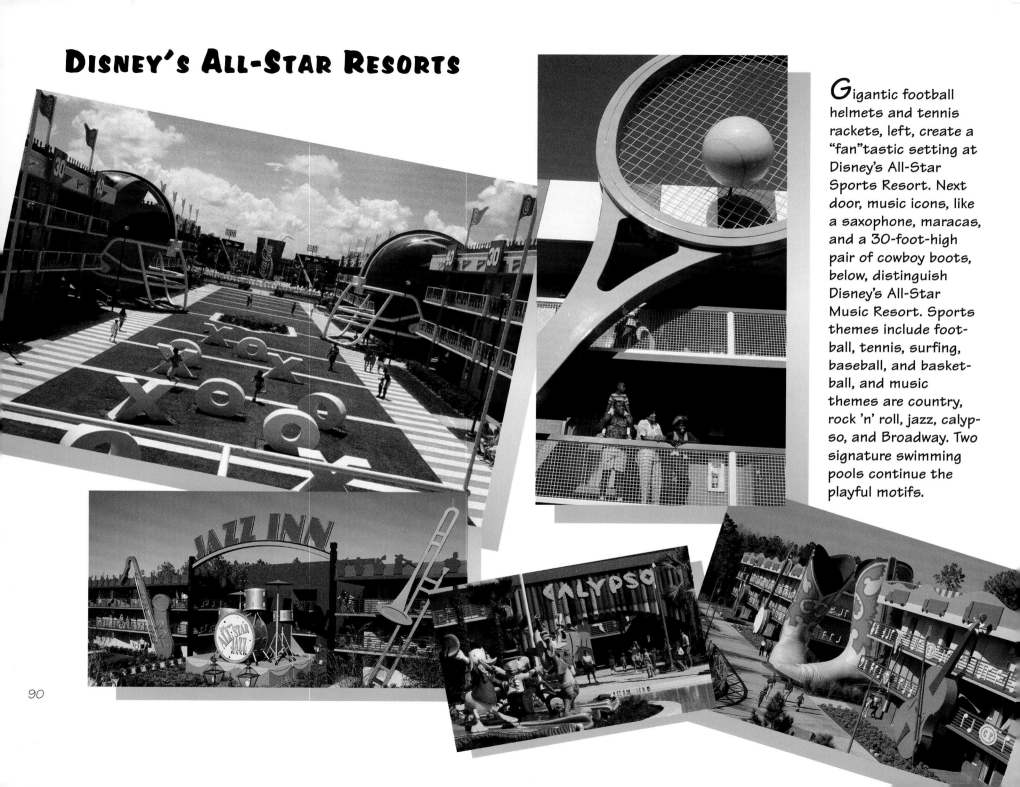

Gigantic football helmets and tennis rackets, left, create a "fan"tastic setting at Disney's All-Star Sports Resort. Next door, music icons, like a saxophone, maracas, and a 30-foot-high pair of cowboy boots, below, distinguish Disney's All-Star Music Resort. Sports themes include football, tennis, surfing, baseball, and basketball, and music themes are country, rock 'n' roll, jazz, calypso, and Broadway. Two signature swimming pools continue the playful motifs.

Disney's Old Key West Resort

With spacious villas and a laid-back atmosphere, this Key West–themed resort is truly a home away from home, part of the Disney Vacation Club (a vacation ownership resort).

Disney Insitute

Ready to stretch your body and your mind? Every day is different—and yours to design—at the Disney Institute, a creative learning community offering an adventure for the mind, body, and soul. You can be as active or relaxed as you like.

Disney's Coronado Springs Resort

You almost expect to see a Spanish conquistador at Disney's newest resort, which draws its inspiration from the grand haciendas and elegant mission cities of the Spanish colonial era. The hotel offers outstanding accommodations for families, as well as a convention center.

93

DISNEY CRUISE LINES

Disney Cruise Line's first ship will set sail on its historic maiden voyage in early 1998, from Port Canaveral, Florida, to the Port of Nassau, and to Disney's Island, Castaway Cay, in the Bahamas.

DISNEY'S ANIMAL KINGDOM™ THEME PARK

The newest Walt Disney World® theme park, opening in Spring 1998, tells the story of all animals—real, imaginary, and extinct—with thrilling attractions, dramatic landscapes, and close encounters with exotic creatures. Home to more than a thousand live animals, Audio-Animatronics creations, and classic characters, the live-action adventure park is based on our endless fascination with animals.

The man-made Tree of Life is the Animal Kingdom's graceful icon, rising 14 stories above Safari Village and carved with a rich tapestry of more than 350 animals.

Above, safari vehicles will take guests for an adventure across the wilds of Africa, with close-up encounters with great herds of animals. Top right, guests can meet animal experts and learn about behind-the-scenes operations at Conservation Station.

Bottom right, The Boneyard playground, an open-air "dig site" for kids, is found at Dinoland USA. Right, dinosaurs roar back to life in the Countdown to Extinction thrill ride. Middle right, Harambe Village, the gateway to Africa.